MW00378393

contents

from the staff

T-shirts, photographs, and autographs—on a quilt, you ask? These things might not be what you think of as "traditional" quilt elements, but for those wanting to honor a special person, to commemorate an event, or to simply preserve the memory of a bygone era, they add a personal touch to a quilt like no other.

Inside, you'll find a variety of memory-themed projects using T-shirts, photos, and autographs in creative ways. And the clear step-by-step instructions and helpful tips for each technique will ensure your quilting success.

enjoy!

t-shirt quilts

Instead of throwing away T-shirts that are outgrown or worn out, salvage the logos and artwork and piece them together to make a unique and memorable quilt.

EVERYONE HAS T-SHIRTS. Perhaps you have favorite T-shirts you've worn for years, a collection of shirts you've received for participating in events, or a pile of shirts you've picked up on your travels. A T-shirt quilt is a great way to turn your stash of shirts into something memorable.

SOME PEOPLE THINK sewing stretchy fabric, such as T-shirt knit, is difficult, but we've made it easy by giving you the secret—fusible tricot interfacing. Without adding a lot of bulk, this lightweight knit interfacing prevents T-shirt knit from stretching out of shape while you're cutting and sewing. Look for interfacing brand names such as So Sheer or Fusi-Knit.

The greatest stretch of most T-shirts goes around the body (crosswise). To stabilize the shirts, place the interfacing so its stretch goes opposite the T-shirt's stretchiest direction. (Usually, this means putting the interfacing's greatest stretch running lengthwise.)

PREPARE T-SHIRTS

1. Cut each T-shirt up the sides and across the top to separate the front and back; remove the sleeves.

2. Cut large rectangles of fusible tricot interfacing several inches larger than is needed for each finished T-shirt piece. This allows for shrinkage or shifting while fusing. Once the T-shirt front or back is interfaced, you'll cut it to the finished size, plus seam allowances, with the logo in the desired position for the finished block.

3. Place each T-shirt front or back wrong side up on your work surface. With the greatest stretch going in opposite directions, place interfacing rectangles fusible side down on the T-shirt pieces. Following the manufacturer's instructions, fuse in place; let cool.

blanket
statement

If you have favorite T-shirts from concerts, sports teams, or other events, you can turn them into a memory-filled quilted keepsake.

DESIGNED BY ELIZABETH TISINGER AND
HANNA PIEPEL
PHOTOGRAPHED BY CAMERON SADEGHPOUR
AND CRAIG ANDERSON

blanket statement

DESIGNER NOTES

Because T-shirt logo size can vary widely, it can be tough to fit them into traditional quilt patterns. Use this to your advantage and design a quilt around a special shirt collection (we used concert T-shirts).

PREPARE T-SHIRTS

Plan which T-shirts you'll use for specific blocks. Referring to Prepare T-shirts on *page 2*, cut up T-shirts and interfacing pieces and apply the interfacing to each T-shirt front or back.

Divide the prepared T-shirts with logos into two piles—a narrow pile (logos that will fit best into a 6"-wide finished row) and a wide pile (logos that will fit better in a 13"-wide finished row). Depending on the size of T-shirts you're using, you may wish to adapt the width of your rows to better accommodate the logos.

CUT LOGO RECTANGLES
from *each* interfaced logo shirt in wide pile, cut:
- 1—14"-wide rectangle, centering logo across width and cutting at least 1" above and below logo where possible

from *each* interfaced logo shirt in narrow pile, cut:
- 1—7"-wide rectangle, centering logo across width and cutting at least 1" above and below logo where possible

CUT REMAINING FABRICS

The quilt top will be assembled in seven vertical rows—four narrow and three wide (see Quilt Assembly Diagram, *right*). To cut the solid-color rectangles you'll need to fill in the spaces between the logo rectangles, refer to the following:

Wide rows: Add heights of 14"-wide logo rectangles (subtracting 1" from each height for seam allowances). Subtract this amount from 250" to get an estimated total amount needed.

Narrow rows: Add heights of 7"-wide logo rectangles (subtracting 1" from each height for seam allowances). Subtract this amount from 350" to get an estimated total amount needed.

from interfaced solid-color plain shirts and scraps of remaining logo shirts, cut:
- Enough 14"-wide rectangles in heights varying from 2" to 6" to equal amount determined above
- Enough 7"-wide rectangles in heights varying from 2" to 20" to equal amount determined above

from solid black, cut:
- 8—2½×42" binding strips

ASSEMBLE QUILT TOP

1. Referring to Quilt Assembly Diagram, *below,* lay out all pieces in seven vertical rows, distributing logo rectangles evenly throughout the rows.

7x75" 14x75" 7x75" 14x75" 7x75" 14x75" 7x75"

Quilt Assembly Diagram

blanket statement

2. Join the pieces in each row using a ½" seam allowance to make four narrow rows and three wide rows. Press all seam allowances open. If necessary, trim each row to 75" long.

3. Join all rows to complete quilt top. Press seam allowances open.

FINISH QUILT

1. Layer the quilt top, batting, and backing according to the instructions in Quilting Basics, which begins on *page 44*.

2. Quilt as desired. Using black thread, machine-quilter Nancy Sharr stitched an allover stipple over the quilt top.

3. Use the solid black 2½×42" binding strips to bind the quilt according to the instructions in Quilting Basics.

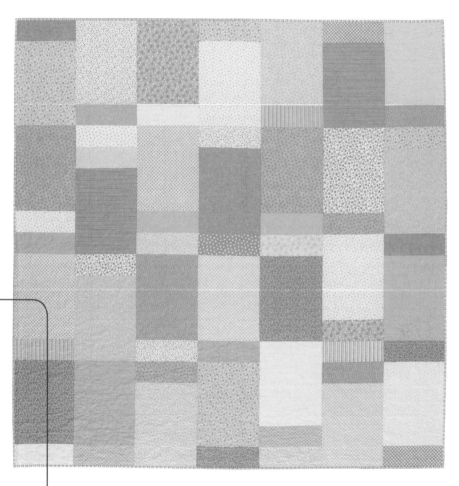

color option

IN THE PINK

If you're not interested in making this quilt from T-shirts, try this fat-quarter-friendly variation of "Blanket Statement," which uses cotton prints in shades of pink. To simplify it even more, we eliminated the narrow rows.

For the 91½×91" quilt, cut 30 fat quarters into 28—13½×17½" rectangles and 35—13½×5" rectangles. Mix and match the rectangles in seven vertical rows of five small rectangles and four large rectangles each, then join the rows with ¼" seams.

remember when

DESIGNED BY HANNA PIEPEL
PHOTOGRAPHED BY PERRY STRUSE

A perfect beginner T-shirt quilt, this easy throw has nine large blocks in which to showcase a few of your favorite T-shirts.

remember when

PREPARE T-SHIRTS

Referring to Prepare T-shirts on *page 2*, cut up T-shirts and interfacing pieces and fuse the interfacing to each T-shirt front or back.

CUT LOGO SQUARES

from *each* interfaced logo shirt, cut:
• 1—12½" square, centering logo and cutting at least 1" above and below logo where possible

CUT REMAINING FABRICS

from tan print, cut:
• 24—2½×12½" sashing rectangles
from blue print, cut:
• 64—2½" squares
• 5—2½×42" binding strips

ASSEMBLE SASHING UNITS

1. For accurate sewing lines, use a quilter's pencil to mark a diagonal line on the wrong side of 48 blue print 2½" squares. (To prevent the fabric from stretching as you draw the lines, place 220-grit sandpaper under the squares.)

2. Align a marked blue print 2½" square with one end of a tan print 2½×12½" sashing rectangle (see Diagram 1; note the placement of the marked diagonal line). Stitch on the marked line; trim away the excess fabric, leaving a ¼" seam allowance. Press the attached triangle open.

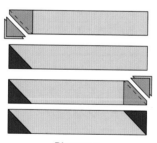

Diagram 1

3. In the same manner, align a second marked blue print 2½" square with the opposite end of the tan print 2½×12½" rectangle (see Diagram 1, again noting the placement of the marked line). Stitch on the marked line; trim and press as before to make a sashing unit. The pieced sashing unit should still measure 2½×12½", including the seam allowances.

4. Repeat steps 2 and 3 to make a total of 24 sashing units.

ASSEMBLE QUILT CENTER

1. Referring to the Quilt Assembly Diagram *opposite*, lay out the nine interfaced logo 12½" squares, the 24 sashing units, and the 16 remaining blue print 2½" squares in seven horizontal rows.

2. Sew together the pieces in each row. Press the seam allowances away from the sashing units.

3. Join the rows to complete the quilt center. Press the seam allowances toward the block rows. The pieced quilt center should measure 41½" square, including the seam allowances.

FINISH QUILT

1. Layer the quilt top, batting, and backing according to the instructions in Quilting Basics, which begins on *page 44*. Quilt as desired.

2. Use the blue print 2½×42" strips to bind the quilt according to the instructions in Quilting Basics.

Use a 12½" square acrylic ruler and a rotary cutter to perfectly center your motifs when cutting logos for "Remember When."

Quilt Assembly Diagram

t-shirt quilt ideas

T-shirt quilts are becoming popular gifts for high school and college graduations. Try making a quilt around a central theme that is important to the recipient. Here's a list of ideas:

- sports
- concerts
- hobbies
- extra-curricular activities
- funny sayings
- favorite charitable events

Or combine a collection of T-shirts with photo transfers (see Photo Transfer Quilts, beginning on *page 31* for instructions). It's a great way to include photos of friends and family for college-bound students.

color option

BLACK-AND-WHITE BEAUTY

Sew a stunning, graphic quilt using striking black-and-white batiks for the large squares and sashing, and an eye-catching red print to create the stars. Make it the focal point of a contemporary loft or apartment by hanging it as a piece of modern art.

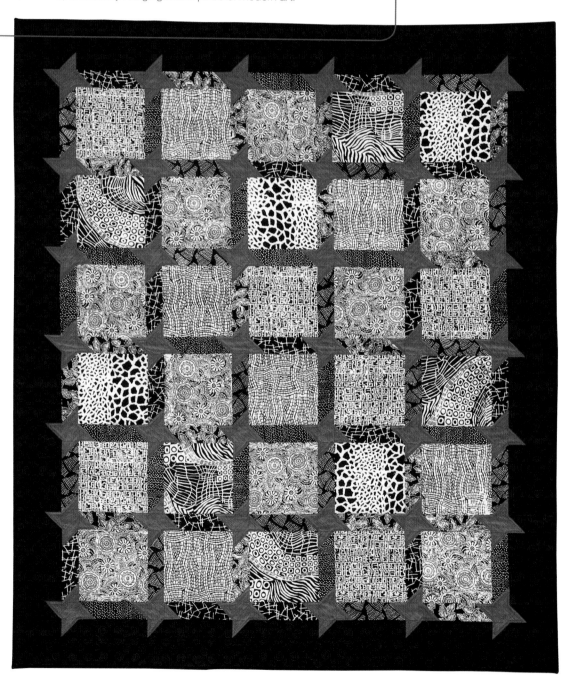

good sports

DESIGNED BY PAULINE RICHARDS
PHOTOGRAPHED BY GREG SCHEIDEMANN

Combine lots of memories in one quilt with this design that has space for T-shirt logos of all sizes.

good sports

MATERIALS

15 to 30 T-shirts with logos
2 yards total of assorted prints in red, blue, and black for blocks
5/8 yard of navy blue print for binding
3 2/3 yards of backing fabric
66×78" of quilt batting
Fusible tricot interfacing

FINISHED QUILT TOP: 60×72"
FINISHED BLOCK: 12" square

Quantities are for 44/45"-wide, 100% cotton fabrics. All measurements include a ¼" seam allowance. Sew with right sides together unless otherwise stated.

DESIGNER NOTES

Every T-shirt quilt is unique due to the vast variety of T-shirts; logos can be on the front, back, or both, and design size will vary widely, especially if you're using shirts acquired over a growing child's lifetime.

Designer Pauline Richards took this into account when designing "Good Sports" and made her quilt with multiple pieced blocks. The different shapes cut for each block allowed her to incorporate T-shirt logos in a wide range of sizes. For each pieced block, she cut pieces from one T-shirt and one coordinating cotton print.

PREPARE T-SHIRTS

Plan which T-shirts you'll use for specific blocks. Referring to Prepare T-shirts on *page 2*, cut up T-shirts and interfacing pieces and fuse the interfacing to each T-shirt front or back.

CUT FABRICS

To make the best use of your fabrics, cut the pieces in the order that follows. (You'll cut the remaining pieces for the quilt in the sections that follow.)

from interfaced T-shirts, cut:
- 15—12½" squares with the largest T-shirt logos centered. ***Note:*** Use a 12½"-square clear acrylic ruler to easily center the designs.

from navy blue print, cut:
- 7—2½×42" binding strips

CUT AND ASSEMBLE FOUR-PATCH BLOCKS

The following instructions make one Four-Patch block. Repeat the cutting and assembly steps to make a total of five Four-Patch blocks.

from one interfaced T-shirt, cut:
- 2—6½" squares, one with a T-shirt logo centered, if desired

from one red, blue, or black print, cut:
- 2—6½" squares

1. Referring to Diagram 1, lay out the four 6½" squares in pairs.

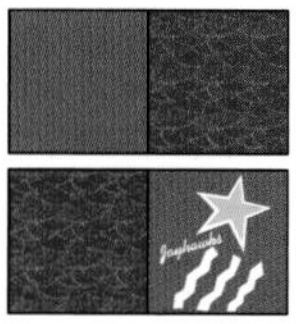

Diagram 1

2. Sew together each pair, pressing the seam allowances toward the red, blue, or black print squares. Join the pairs to make a Four-Patch block. Press the seam allowance in one direction. The pieced Four-Patch block should measure 12½" square, including the seam allowances.

good sports

CUT AND ASSEMBLE THREE-BAR BLOCKS

The following instructions make one three-bar block. Repeat the cutting and assembly steps to make a total of four three-bar blocks.

from one interfaced T-shirt, cut:
• 1—4½×12½" rectangle, with a T-shirt logo centered, if desired
from one red, blue, or black print, cut:
• 2—4½×12½" rectangles

1. Referring to Diagram 2, lay out the three 4½×12½" rectangles.

Diagram 2

2. Sew together the pieces to make a three-bar block. Press the seam allowances toward the red, blue, or black print rectangles. The pieced three-bar block should measure 12½" square, including the seam allowances.

CUT AND ASSEMBLE FLYING GEESE BLOCKS

The following instructions make one Flying Geese block. Repeat the cutting and assembly steps to make a total of four Flying Geese blocks.

The Triangle Pattern is *opposite.* To make a template of the pattern, follow the instructions in Quilting Basics, which begins on *page 44.*

from one interfaced T-shirt, cut:
• 2 of Triangle Pattern, one with a T-shirt logo centered, if desired
from one red, blue, or black print, cut:
• 2—6⅞" squares, cutting each in half diagonally for a total of four small triangles

1. Sew a red, blue, or black print small triangle to a short edge of a T-shirt triangle (see Diagram 3). **Note:** The corner of the small triangle will extend beyond the point of the T-shirt triangle.

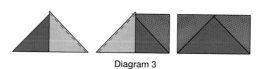

Diagram 3

2. Press the attached small triangle open, pressing the seam allowance toward the small triangle.

3. In the same manner, join a second red, blue, or black print small triangle to the T-shirt triangle. Press the small triangle open to make a Flying Geese unit. The pieced Flying Geese unit should measure 6½×12½", including the seam allowances.

4. Repeat steps 1 through 3 to make two Flying Geese units.

5. Join the two Flying Geese units to make a Flying Geese block (see Diagram 4). Press the seam allowance in one direction. The pieced Flying Geese block should measure 12½" square, including the seam allowances.

Diagram 4

CUT AND ASSEMBLE HOURGLASS BLOCKS

The following instructions make one hourglass block. Repeat the cutting and assembly steps to make two hourglass blocks.

from one interfaced T-shirt, cut:
• 2 of Triangle Pattern, one with a T-shirt logo centered, if desired
from one red, blue, or black print, cut:
• 2 of Triangle Pattern

1. Referring to Diagram 5, lay out the four triangles in pairs.

2. Sew together each pair, pressing the seam allowances toward the red, blue, or black print triangles. Join the pairs to make an hourglass block. Press the seam allowance in one direction. The pieced hourglass block should measure 12½" square, including the seam allowances.

Diagram 5

ASSEMBLE QUILT TOP

1. Referring to the Quilt Assembly Diagram for placement, lay out the 15 T-shirt 12½" squares, the five Four-Patch blocks, the four Three-Bar blocks, the four Flying Geese blocks, and the two Hourglass blocks in six horizontal rows.

2. Sew together the pieces in each row. To reduce bulk, press the seam allowances in each row away from the T-shirt 12½" squares.

3. Join the pieced rows to complete the quilt top. Press the seam allowances in one direction.

FINISH QUILT

1. Layer the quilt top, batting, and backing according to the instructions in Quilting Basics, which begins on *page 44*.

2. Quilt as desired. Machine-quilter Nancy Sharr stitched a meandering pattern with stars and loops all over the quilt.

3. Use the navy blue print 2½×42" strips to bind the quilt according to the instructions in Quilting Basics.

Quilt Assembly Diagram

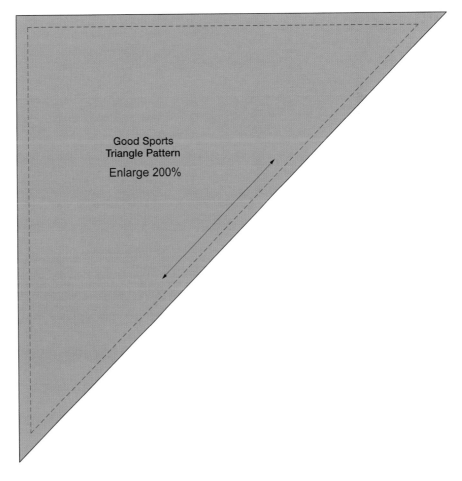

Good Sports
Triangle Pattern
Enlarge 200%

good sports

color option

CUDDLE UP

In lieu of the four different pieced blocks used in "Good Sports," simplify by alternating just one pieced block with T-shirt squares. The Four-Patch blocks in the throw-size quilt *below* utilize pile fabric. Because this soft, textured fabric is very sensitive to heat, avoid touching it with an iron; finger-press seams instead.

Pile fabrics, often used for making stuffed animals or baby quilts, are available in quilt shops under a variety of brand names. One version, Oh So Soft from AvLyn Inc., was used for this quilt's backing, resulting in a luxurious throw.

autograph quilts

Remember the names of family members, close friends, or attendees at a special event with a quilt that showcases their signatures. Hand out individual blocks to each person to sign. For extra personalization, ask each person to choose a fabric and stitch up a block for the quilt.

BEFORE PUTTING PEN TO FABRIC, follow these tips to ensure your success. By using the proper tools and with careful preparation, you'll be rewarded with years of durability.

CHOOSE SMOOTH-SURFACE, 100% cotton fabrics and always prewash them. Cotton fabrics usually contain sizing, which acts as a barrier to ink penetration.

SELECT A FABRIC COLOR that will allow the ink to show. Avoid white-on-white prints because the pattern is painted onto the fabric rather than dyed into it. The paint makes writing difficult and the ink doesn't penetrate as well.

USE PENS that have permanent ink and are made for fabric. A fine point (.01) writes delicately and is less likely to bleed as it writes. Lines can be made thicker by going over them more than once. For larger letters or numbers, a .05-diameter pen works well.

TEST THE PEN AND FABRIC together. Write slowly and with a lighter touch than you would normally use to write on paper. This allows time for the ink to flow into the fabric and lets you control the letters. Write on a fabric sample; then follow the manufacturer's directions (if included) for setting the ink. Wait 24 hours for the ink to set and then wash the sample as you would any fine quilt.

STABILIZE THE FABRIC and create guidelines with freezer paper. Cut a piece of freezer paper large enough to cover the fabric's writing area. Use a ruler and thick black marker to draw evenly spaced lines on the freezer paper's dull side. Iron the freezer paper to the fabric's wrong side with a hot, dry iron. Repeat to make several samples for practice.

quilt of prayers

Wrap a friend or family member in a quilt containing encouraging words of comfort. Each person can write a message on one of the machine-appliquéd hearts to help speed his or her recovery.

DESIGNED BY JACKIE MUEHLSTEIN AND
JANET NEWSOM
PHOTOGRAPHED BY MARCIA CAMERON
AND STEVE STRUSE

MATERIALS

4½ yards total of assorted scraps for blocks

4½ yards of muslin

2¾ yards of burgundy print for setting squares, borders, and sashing

6 yards of 22"-wide fusible web

74×92" of quilt batting

5¼ yards of backing fabric

FINISHED QUILT TOP: 68x86"

FNISHED BLOCK: 14½" square

Quantities specified for 44/45"-wide, 100% cotton fabrics. All measurements include a ¼" seam allowance. Sew with right sides together unless otherwise stated.

CUT FABRICS

To make the best use of your fabrics, cut the pieces in the order that follows. Cut border strips lengthwise (parallel to the selvage).

To make templates of the pattern, found on *page 20*, follow the instructions in Quilting Basics, which begins on *page 44*.

1. Lay fusible web, paper side up, over the pattern. With a pencil, trace the pattern the number of times indicated in cutting instructions. Cut out the pieces roughly ¼" outside of the traced lines.

2. Following the manufacturer's instructions, press the fusible-web shapes onto the wrong side of the muslin. Let the fabric cool. Cut out the shapes on the drawn lines. Peel off the paper backings.

from assorted scraps, cut:
• 112—5½×9½" rectangles
from muslin, cut:
• 112 of Heart Pattern
from burgundy print, cut:
• 10—2½×42" strips for binding
• 2—3×84½" inner border strips
• 2—3¼×61½" top and bottom border strips
• 24—4½" setting squares
• 14—3×5½" sashing strips for borders

ASSEMBLE AND APPLIQUE HEART UNITS

1. Place an appliqué piece on an assorted scrap 5½×9½" rectangle. Fuse the piece in place with a hot, dry iron (or, if different, use the iron temperature recommended in the manufacturer's instructions) to make an appliquéd heart unit. Repeat to make a total of 112 appliquéd heart units.

2. Machine-blanket-stitch around each appliquéd heart.

ASSEMBLE BRIGHT HOPES BLOCKS

1. Place an appliquéd heart unit along the top edge of a burgundy print 4½" square. Sew together, stopping 1" from the top left corner (see Diagram 1) to make a Step 1 unit. Press the seam allowance toward the dark print rectangle.

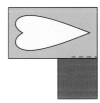

Diagram 1

2. Sew an appliquéd heart unit to the right-hand edge of the Step 1 unit. Press the seam allowance toward the dark print rectangle. Then join another appliquéd heart unit to the bottom edge (see Diagram 2) to make a Step 2 unit. Press the seam allowance toward the dark print rectangle.

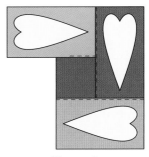

Diagram 2

3. Add a fourth appliquéd heart unit to the left-hand edge of the Step 2 unit. Sew the remaining portion of the first dark print rectangle in place (see Diagram 3) to make a Bright Hopes block. The finished Bright Hopes block should measure 14½" square, including the seam allowances.

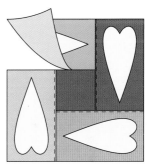

Diagram 3

4. Repeat steps 1 through 3 to make a total of 24 Bright Hopes blocks (see Diagram 4).

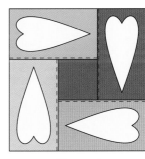

Diagram 4

quilt of prayers

ASSEMBLE QUILT CENTER

Referring to the photograph *opposite,* lay out the Bright Hopes blocks in six horizontal rows. Sew together the pieces in each row. Press the seam allowances in opposite directions. Then join the rows to complete the quilt center. Press the seam allowances in opposite directions. The pieced quilt center should measure 56½×84½", including the seam allowances.

ASSEMBLE AND ADD BORDERS

1. Center and sew one dark print 3×84½" inner border strip to each side edge of the pieced quilt center. Then center and add a dark print 3¼×61½" border strip to the top and bottom edges of the pieced quilt center. Press all seam allowances toward the dark print inner border.

2. Referring to the photograph *opposite* for placement, lay out one heart border strip, alternating eight appliquéd heart units and seven burgundy print 3×5½" sashing strips in one vertical row. Sew together along the 5½" edges. Press the seam allowances in one direction. The pieced strip should measure 5½×90", including the seam allowances. Repeat to make a second heart border strip. Add the side outer border strips to opposite edges of the pieced quilt center.

FINISH QUILT

1. Layer the quilt top, batting, and backing according to the instructions in Quilting Basics, which begins on *page 44.* Quilt as desired.

2. Use the burgundy print 2½×42" strips to bind the quilt according to the instructions in Quilting Basics.

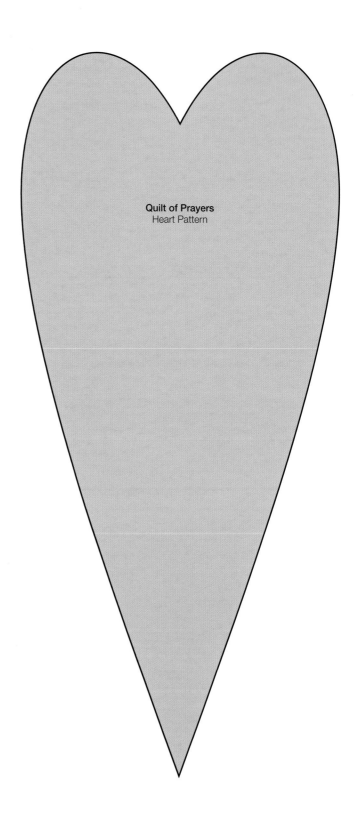

Quilt of Prayers
Heart Pattern

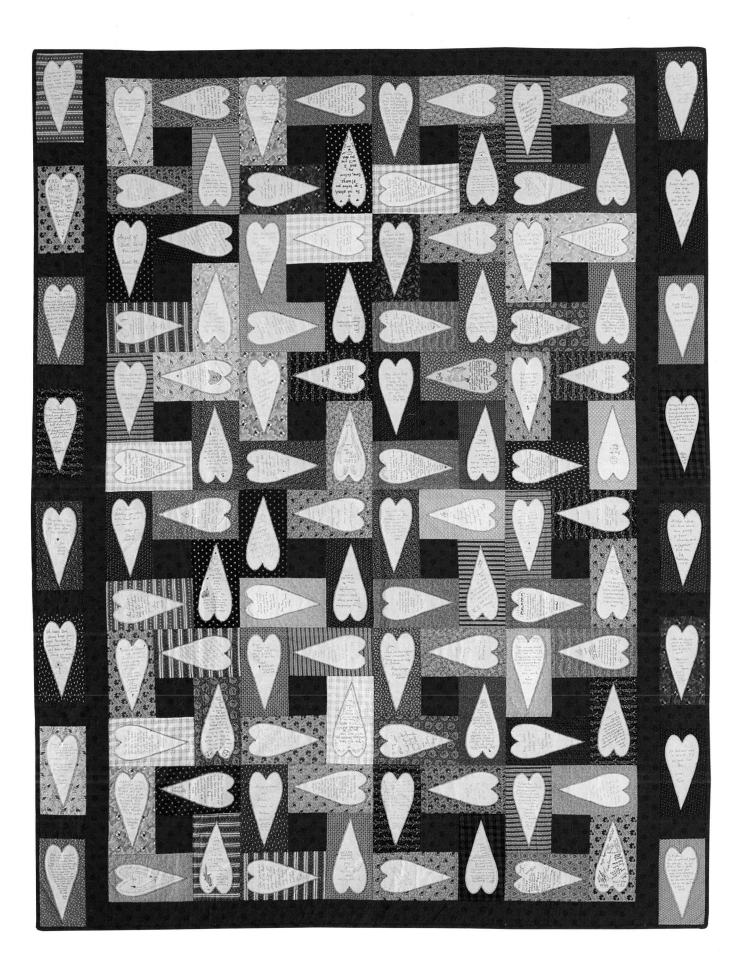

quilting stars

DESIGNED BY
LILA SCOTT
PHOTOGRAPHED BY
PERRY STRUSE AND
STEVE STRUSE

If you're looking for a gift for a few quilting friends or just a quilt to remember a special group of people, the Chimney Sweep blocks on this red-white-and-blue quilt make perfect spots for handwritten signatures.

MATERIALS

- 9—⅛-yard pieces of assorted blue prints for signature blocks
- 1 yard of blue star print for 54-40 or Fight blocks and binding
- 1⅛ yards of blue moon print for setting triangles and outer border
- 9—⅛-yard pieces of assorted red prints for signature blocks
- ¼ yard of red star print No. 1 for 54-40 or Fight blocks
- ¾ yard of red star print No. 2 for Nine-Patch blocks
- 1⅛ yards of white print for signature blocks
- 1⅛ yards of white star print for Nine-Patch and 54-40 or Fight blocks
- 3¼ yards of backing fabric
- 58×70" piece of quilt batting

FINISHED QUILT TOP: 51½×63½"
FINISHED SIGNATURE BLOCK:
  8½" square
FINISHED 54-40 or FIGHT BLOCK:
  6" square
FINISHED NINE-PATCH BLOCK:
  6" square

Quantities specified for 44/45"-wide, 100% cotton fabrics. All measurements include a ¼" seam allowance unless otherwise stated.

CUT FABRICS

To make the best use of your fabrics, cut the pieces in the order that follows. The border strip lengths are mathematically correct. You may wish to cut the strips longer than specified to allow for possible sewing differences. Trim the border strips to the correct length for your quilt center before adding them.

To make templates of the patterns found on *page 26*, follow the instructions in Quilting Basics, which begins on *page 44*.

from *each* of the nine assorted blue prints, cut:
- 1—2×42" strip
- 8—2" squares or 8 of Pattern A

from blue star print, cut:
- 6—2½×42" binding strips
- 3—1½×42" strips
- 32 each of patterns E and E reversed

from blue moon print, cut:
- 6—2¼×42" strips for outer border
- 3—13⅜" squares, cutting each diagonally twice in an X for a total of 12 side setting triangles (you'll have 2 leftover triangles)
- 2—7" squares, cutting each in half diagonally for a total of 4 corner setting triangles

from *each* of the assorted red prints, cut:
- 1—2×42" strip

from red star print No. 1, cut:
- 3—1½×42" strips

from red star print No. 2, cut:
- 9—2½×42" strips

from white print, cut:
- 36—2" squares or 36 of Pattern A
- 18—2×5" rectangles or 18 of Pattern B
- 54—3⅜" squares, cutting each diagonally twice in an X for a total of 216 triangles, or 216 of Pattern C
- 36—2" squares, cutting each in half diagonally for a total of 72 triangles, or 72 of Pattern D

from white star print, cut:
- 9—2½×42" strips
- 32 of Pattern F

ASSEMBLE SIGNATURE BLOCKS

1. Aligning long edges, sew together one blue print 2×42" strip and one red print 2×42" strip to make a strip set (see Diagram 1). Press the seam allowance toward the blue print strip. Cut the strip set into 2"-wide segments for a total of 16.

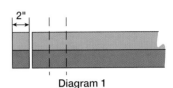

Diagram 1

2. Referring to Diagram 2 for placement, lay out eight 2"-wide segments, four A squares of the same blue print, two white print A squares, one white print B rectangle, 12 white print C triangles, and four white print D triangles.

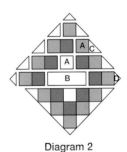

Diagram 2

3. Sew together the pieces in each row, except for the white print D triangles. Press the seam allowances toward the blue print squares. Then join the rows, adding the white print D triangles last, to make one signature block. The pieced signature block should measure 9" square, including the seam allowances.

4. Repeat steps 2 and 3 to make an identical block.

5. Repeat steps 1 thorough 4 to make a total of 18 signature blocks (nine pairs).

quilting stars

ASSEMBLE QUILT CENTER

1. Referring to the Quilt Assembly Diagram, lay out the 18 signature blocks, 10 blue moon print side setting triangles, and four blue moon print corner setting triangles in diagonal rows.

2. Sew together the pieces in each row, except for the corner setting triangles. Press the seam allowances in one direction, alternating the direction with each row. Then join the rows, adding the corner setting triangles last, to complete the quilt center. Press the seam allowances in one direction. The pieced quilt center should measure 36½x48½", including seam allowances.

Quilt Assembly Diagram

ASSEMBLE 54-40 OR FIGHT BLOCKS

1. Aligning long edges, sew together one blue star print 1½x42" strip and one red star print No. 1—1½x42" strip to make a strip set (see Diagram 3, *above middle*). Press the seam allowance toward the blue print strip. Repeat to make a total of three strip sets. Cut the strips sets into 1½"-wide segments for a total of 80.

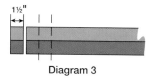

Diagram 3

2. Referring to Diagram 4, sew together two 1½"-wide segments to make a Four-Patch unit. Press the seam allowance in one direction. The pieced Four-Patch unit should measure 2½"-square, including the seam allowances. Repeat to make a total of 40 Four-Patch units.

Diagram 4

3. Sew a blue star print E triangle and a blue star print E reversed triangle to each long side of a white star print F triangle to make a star point unit (see Diagram 5). Press the seam allowances toward the blue star print triangles. Repeat to make a total of 32 star point units.

Diagram 5

4. Referring to Diagram 6, lay out five Four-Patch units and four star point units in three horizontal rows. Sew together the squares in each row. Press the seam allowances toward the star point units. Then join the rows to make a 54-40 or Fight block. Press the seam allowances in one direction. The pieced 54-40 or Fight block should measure 6½" square, including the seam allowances. Repeat to make a total of eight 54-40 or Fight blocks.

Diagram 6

ASSEMBLE NINE-PATCH BLOCKS

1. Aligning long edges, sew two red star print No. 2—2½x42" strips to a white star print 2½x42" strip to make a strip set A (see Diagram 7). Press the seam allowances toward the red print strips. Repeat for a total of three of strip set A. Cut the strip sets into 2½"-wide segments for total of 38.

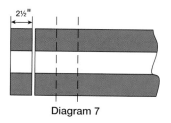

Diagram 7

2. In the same manner, sew two white star print 2½x42" strips to a red star print 2½x42" strip to make strip set B (see Diagram 8). Press the seam allowances toward the red print strip. Repeat for a total of three of strip set B. Cut the strip sets into 2½"-wide segments for a total of 34.

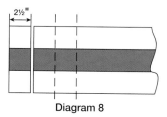

Diagram 8

3. Referring to Diagram 9, sew together two strip set A segments and one strip set B segment to make a Nine-Patch block A. Press the seam allowances in one direction. Pieced Nine-Patch block A should measure 6½" square, including the seam allowances. Repeat to make a total of 14 of Nine-Patch block A.

Diagram 9

Diagram 10

4. Referring to Diagram 10, *opposite,* sew together one strip set A segment and two strip set B segments to make a Nine-Patch block B. Press the seam allowances in one direction. Pieced Nine-Patch block B should measure 6½" square, including the seam allowances. Repeat to make a total of 10 of Nine-Patch block B.

ASSEMBLE AND ADD PIECED BORDER

1. Referring to Diagram 11, lay out two 54-40 or Fight blocks, three of Nine-Patch block A, and three of Nine-Patch block B. Note the direction of the red squares in the 54-40 or Fight blocks. Sew together the squares to make a side pieced border strip. Repeat to make a second side pieced border strip.

Sew the side pieced border strips to the side edges of the pieced quilt center, carefully noting the placement of the 54-40 or Fight blocks.

2. Referring to Diagram 12, lay out two 54-40 or Fight blocks, four of Nine-Patch block A, and two of Nine-Patch block B. Note the direction of the red squares in the 54-40 or Fight blocks. Sew together the squares to make the top pieced border strip. Repeat to make the bottom pieced border strip.

3. Sew the pieced border strips to the top and bottom edges of the pieced quilt center, carefully noting the placement of the 54-40 or Fight blocks. The pieced quilt center should now measure 48½×60½", including the seam allowances.

ADD OUTER BORDERS

1. Cut and piece the blue moon print 2¼×42" strips to make the following:
- 2—2¼×60½" outer border strips
- 2—2¼×52" outer border strips

2. Sew one blue moon print 2¼×60½" outer border strip to each side edge of the pieced quilt center. Then join a blue moon print 2¼×52" outer border strip to the top and bottom edges of the pieced quilt center to complete the quilt top. Press all seam allowances toward the blue moon print outer border.

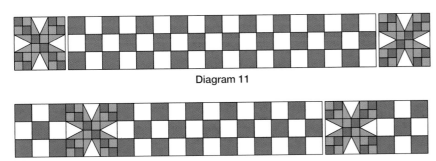

Diagram 11

Diagram 12

quilting stars

FINISH THE QUILT

1. Layer the quilt top, batting, and backing according to the instructions in Quilting Basics, which begins on *page 44*.

2. Quilt as desired. Lila machine-quilted diagonally through the blue squares of the signature blocks and stipple-quilted in the red and white squares, leaving the center rectangles clear for signatures. She quilted in the ditch around the outside of the signature blocks and the 54-40 or Fight blocks. She stipple-quilted the blue borders and quilted diagonally through the checkerboard in the border.

3. Use the blue star print 2½×42" strips to bind the quilt according to the instructions in Quilting Basics.

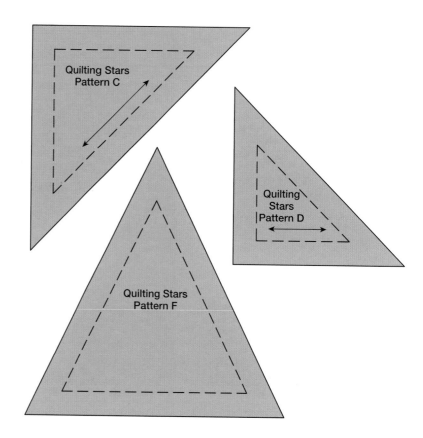

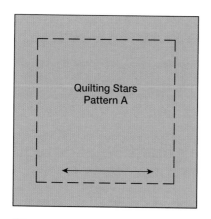

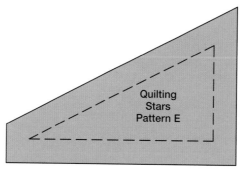

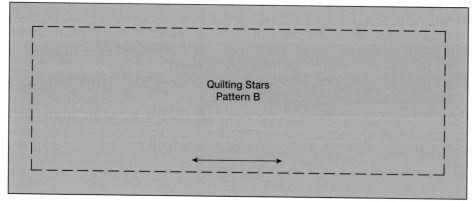

crowded lake

DESIGNED BY KRIS KERRIGAN
PHOTOGRAPHED BY
PERRY STRUSE AND
MARCIA CAMERON

To make this simple signature wall hanging, first hand out strips of fabric backed with freezer paper to friends. Next, sew the signed strips into simple patchwork blocks that resemble a throng of canoes filling a waterfront.

crowded lake

MATERIALS

⅓ yard of light blue print for blocks

⅛ yard *each* of 16 assorted dark gold, red, blue, brown, green, and purple homespun plaids and stripes for blocks and outer border

⅛ yard *each* of 16 assorted light cream and tan homespun plaids, solids, and stripes for blocks and outer border

¼ yard of medium brown stripe for inner border

¼ yard medium brown check for binding

36" square of backing fabric

36" square of quilt batting

Black fine-tip permanent marker

Freezer paper

Taupe perle cotton

FINISHED QUILT TOP: 30" square
FINISHED BLOCK: 6" square

Quantities specified for 44/45"-wide, 100% cotton fabrics. All measurements include a ¼" seam allowance unless otherwise stated.

CUT FABRICS

To make the best use of your fabrics, cut the pieces in the order that follows. There are no pattern pieces; the letter designations are for placement only.

from light blue print, cut:
• 16—3⅞" squares, cutting each in half diagonally for a total of 32 triangles for position C

from *each* of the 16 assorted dark gold, red, blue, brown, green, and purple homespun plaids and stripes, cut:
• 2—1⅞×4¾" rectangles for position B
• 1—3⅞" square, cutting it in half diagonally for a total of 2 triangles for position C
• 7—1½×2½" rectangles for position E for border (You'll only use 104 of the 112 rectangles)

from one remaining dark brown homespun plaid, cut:
• 4—2½" squares for position F

from *each* of the 16 assorted light cream and tan homespun plaids, solids, and stripes, cut:
• 1—2×4¾" rectangle for position A

from remaining assorted light cream and tan homespun plaids, solids, and stripes, cut:
• 224—1½" squares for position D

from medium brown stripe, cut:
• 2—1½×26½" inner border strips
• 2—1½×24½" inner border strips

from medium brown check, cut:
• 3—2½×42" binding strips

from freezer paper, cut:
• 16—1½×4¼" rectangles

CREATE SIGNATURE STRIPS

1. Center the shiny side of a freezer paper 1½×4¼" rectangle facing the wrong side of a light cream or tan 2×4¾" rectangle; press. Repeat with the remaining 15 freezer-paper strips and light cream or tan rectangles.

2. Using the black fine-tip permanent marker, have friends sign the fabric side of the prepared strips, making sure they don't write in the seam allowance. Remove the freezer paper once the strips are signed. (Project designer Kris Kerrigan recommends preparing a few extra strips in case someone makes a mistake.)

ASSEMBLE SIGNATURE BLOCKS

1. For one block you'll need one light cream or tan signature A strip, two light blue print C triangles, and one set of two B rectangles and two C triangles in the same dark homespun plaid or stripe.

2. Aligning long edges, sew one dark homespun plaid or stripe B rectangle to each long edge of the light cream or tan signature A strip (see Diagram 1) to make the block center. Press the seam allowances toward the dark rectangles. The pieced block center should measure 4¾" square, including seam allowances.

Diagram 1

3. Referring to Diagram 2 for placement, sew a dark homespun plaid or stripe C triangle to each side edge of the block center. Press the seam allowances toward the dark triangles.

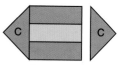

Diagram 2

4. Sew the light blue print C triangles to the top and bottom edges of the block center (see Diagram 3). Press the seam allowances toward the light triangles. The pieced block should measure 6½" square, including the seam allowances.

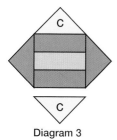

Diagram 3

5. Repeat steps 1 through 3 to make a total of 16 signature blocks.

ASSEMBLE QUILT TOP

Referring to the photograph at *right* for placement, lay out the 16 signature blocks in four horizontal rows of four blocks each. Sew together the blocks in each row. Press the seam allowances in each row in one direction, alternating the direction with each row. Then join the rows. Press the seam allowances in one direction. The pieced quilt top should measure 24½" square, including the seam allowances.

ADD INNER BORDER

1. Sew one medium brown stripe 1½×24½" inner border strip to the top edge and one to the bottom edge of the pieced quilt top. Press the seam allowances toward the border.

2. Add a medium brown stripe 1½×26½" inner border strip to each side edge of the pieced quilt top. Press the seam allowances toward the border.

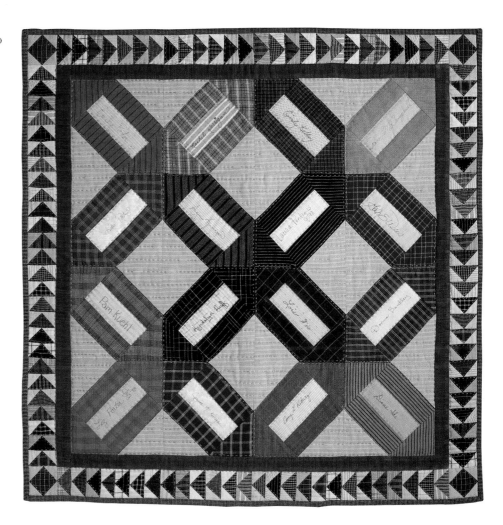

ASSEMBLE AND ADD OUTER BORDER

1. For accurate sewing lines, use a quilting pencil to mark the 224 light cream or tan homespun plaid, solid, or stripe D squares with a diagonal line on the wrong side of the fabric. (To prevent your fabric from stretching as you draw the lines, place 220-grit sandpaper under the squares.)

2. With right sides together, align one marked light cream or tan D square with one end of a dark plaid or stripe E rectangle (see Diagram 4; note the placement of the sewing line). Stitch on the sewing line. Trim the seam allowance

to ¼". Press open the attached light triangle. In the same manner, sew a second marked light cream or tan D square to the opposite end of the dark E rectangle; trim and press open to complete a Flying Geese unit. The pieced Flying Geese unit should measure 1½×2½", including the seam allowances.

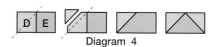

Diagram 4

3. Repeat Step 2 for a total of 104 Flying Geese units.

4. With right sides together, align one marked light cream or tan D square with one corner of a dark brown homespun plaid F square (see Diagram 5; note the placement of the sewing line). Stitch on the sewing line. Trim the seam allowance to ¼". Press open the attached light triangle. In the same manner, sew a marked light cream or tan D square to each of the remaining corners of the dark F square; trim and press open after adding each triangle to complete a corner unit. The pieced corner unit should measure 2½" square, including the seam allowances.

Diagram 5

5. Repeat Step 4 to make a total of four corner units.

6. Aligning long raw edges, sew together 26 Flying Geese units in a horizontal row to make the top outer border strip (see the photograph on *page 29* for placement). Press the seam allowances open. Repeat to make the bottom outer border strip. Add the outer border strips to the top and bottom edges of the pieced quilt top. Press the seam allowances toward inner border.

7. Aligning long raw edges, sew together 26 Flying Geese units in a vertical row to make a side outer border strip (see the photograph on *page 29* for placement). Press the seam allowances open. Sew a corner unit to each end of the strip. Press the seam allowances toward the corner units. Repeat to make a second side outer border strip. Add the side outer border strips to the side edges of the pieced quilt top. Press the seam allowances toward the inner border.

FINISH QUILT

1. Layer the quilt top, batting, and backing according to the instructions in Quilting Basics, which begins on *page 44*.

2. Quilt as desired. Kris used taupe perle cotton and long, primitive stitches to hand-quilt in the ditch just inside the outside edges of each block, signature strip, Flying Geese triangle, and corner unit. Kris also quilted horizontal lines on each light blue print triangle to resemble water ripples.

3. Use the medium brown check 2½×42" strips to bind the quilt according to the instructions in Quilting Basics.

color option

CRISSCROSSED ARROWS

Instead of seeing canoes in the block as designer Kris Kerrigan did, quilt tester Laura Boehnke saw arrows. By simply placing red or blue fabrics in the center of the signature strip and in the triangles at either end of the strip, Laura designed an arrow. Then she alternated the direction of red and blue arrows in the horizontal and vertical rows to create a pattern of crisscrossing red and blue arrows.

photo quilts

Give a quilt a personalized twist by embellishing it with your own photo-transferred images.

NEARY EVERYONE has boxes and albums filled with photographs, memorabilia, artwork, clippings, and other cherished mementos. But instead of keeping those keepsakes tucked away, learn how to heat-transfer the images onto fabric to make a treasured quilt for a gift or as a family heirloom.

STEP 1: SELECT YOUR THEME AND PROJECT

Weddings and anniversaries, birthdays, special vacations, graduations, retirements, family histories, pets, and childhood memories are popular themes for projects. Although quilted wall hangings are the most popular project for this technique, pillows, bags, Christmas ornaments, and wearables also work.

STEP 2: CHOOSE PHOTOS AND ARTWORK

Obviously, photographs leap to mind when we think of photo transfers. But despite the name, photo-transfer techniques are not limited to photos. Artwork, letters, certificates, and copyright-free art (also known as clip art) are good sources too, and small, nonpaper objects, such as old linens and jewelry, also can be laid directly on the scanner or photocopier glass. As a rule, choose items that will fit onto the scanner or photocopier glass. Keep in mind that any three-dimensional objects will become one-dimensional when they're copied onto photo-transfer paper.

STEP 3: SELECT THE FABRICS

Careful fabric selection is key to a successful photo transfer. White cotton is the most frequently used surface for photo-transferring, because it tends to brighten and add highlights to images. Tan and ivory tend to tone down images but can lend wonderful rustic or nostalgic effects. For the best-quality photo transfers, choose sateens and pima cottons; their tightly woven fibers produce excellent results, making them especially desirable for photographs of people. Always prewash the fabrics to avoid shrinkage and later distortion of the images.

Make a big impact with your photo transfers by grouping them in a series to tell a story.

photo quilts

Experiment with textured and subtly patterned fabrics to add interest to your creations. Search beyond conventional fabrics for inspiration, too, such as leather.

STEP 4: CHOOSE A PHOTO-TRANSFER METHOD

The easiest way to transfer a photo to fabric is to use iron-on photo transfer paper. The most popular papers use either a color printer or a color photocopier to print the photo onto the paper. When choosing a method, consider what's available to you—if you have a color printer at home and many digital photos on your computer, papers made for color printers may be most convenient. But if you're working with color prints, papers made for color photocopiers might be the right choice for you.

With so many people using digital cameras today, transfer paper made specifically for ink-jet, bubble, or laser printers is a convenient way to print photos and text directly from your computer to transfer paper. Many printer manufacturers market papers specifically for their brand, but the main thing to look for is the type of printer that the paper is compatible with. Using a computer to print your images and text gives you the most flexibility, allowing you to enhance, crop, and enlarge your photos as desired.

If you choose transfer paper suitable for photocopying, it's essential to have access to a color photocopier. Most copy centers have color photocopiers, and for a small fee, will copy images onto your photo-transfer paper. If you want to copy black-and-white images, don't use a black-and-white photocopier—it can get too hot and may melt the photo-transfer paper. Instead, make a black-and-white photocopy on a color photocopier.

STEP 5: HEAT-TRANSFERRING IMAGES ONTO FABRIC

When using heat-transfer paper, it's important to follow the manufacturer's instructions for transferring the images to fabric. Usually, an iron or a heat press (commonly found in T-shirt shops) is necessary to transfer the image; however, the instructions often differ as to when to peel away the paper backing. Some brands may require removal of the paper while the image is still hot, while other papers work best after the fabric has cooled.

STEP 6: TRIM PHOTOS AND ADD BORDERS

You can leave a white edge around your photo for a border or add a fabric border.

If you add a fabric border, leave a scant ¼" seam allowance so no white fabric will show through after you've added the fabric border.

STEP 7: DESIGN YOUR PROJECT

Once your images are framed, move them around on a vertical design wall with any other quilt blocks, sashing strips, and other elements of your quilt design until the arrangement pleases you. Stand back and squint at your design—you should see your photos first. Simple, traditional block patterns often show off photo transfers best without competing with the images.

STEP 8: QUILT AS DESIRED

Generally, quilting is not done through transferred photos. Some quilters prefer to quilt around faces, while others like to add appliqué or embroidery for a finishing touch.

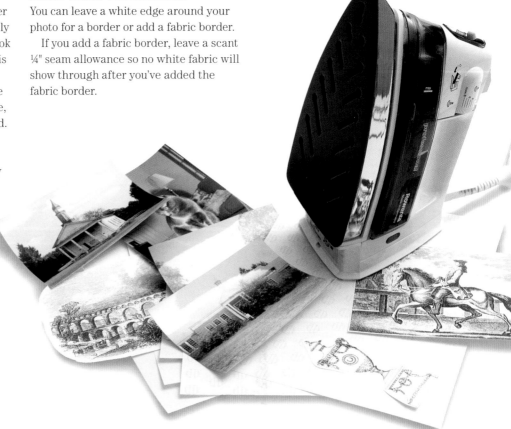

HOW TO TRANSFER AN IMAGE WITH A PHOTOCOPIER

1. To make the most economical use of your transfer paper, lay as many images or objects onto the print area of the photocopier's glass surface as will fit (*photo 1*). Or tape your images onto a sheet of white paper in advance, which will tell you how much transfer paper you'll need to take with you to the copy center. Don't worry about cropping your photographs—you can trim the photocopied transfer paper later without damaging your original images.

2. Manually feed the photo-transfer paper into the copier one sheet at a time, placing the paper in the machine's bypass tray. Be sure to place the paper so it will copy onto the transfer side of the paper—follow the manufacturer's instructions carefully and follow the recommendations for printer settings.

3. After you've copied the images onto the paper, use scissors to cut the images apart. If you want to crop any of the images, cut away any unwanted areas at this time.

4. Choose a hard pressing surface, such as a countertop or a large hard-cover book. A padded ironing board won't produce good results—you'll need a firm surface that will let the color saturate the fabric. Lay a towel over the surface and lay your fabric on top of the towel. With the image facing down, place the transfer-paper image on the fabric.

5. Using an iron at the hottest setting and without steam, press the iron firmly on the paper side of the image (*photo 2*). Press and hold the iron following the paper manufacturer's instructions; then lift and press another area of the paper. Continue pressing until you've covered all areas of the paper. Follow the manufacturer's instructions to peel off the paper when the paper is still hot or when it's cool.

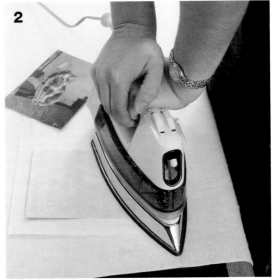

HOW TO TRANSFER AN IMAGE WITH A COLOR PRINTER

1. Choose a paper compatible to the type of printer you have, such as ink-jet, bubble jet, or laser printers, and follow the paper manufacturer's guidelines for the necessary printer resolution for optimal photo-transfer results.

2. Set your printer at the highest-quality setting. For the best image, always sacrifice the highest speed setting for the best-quality setting.

3. If printing text, use your software capabilities to print the text in reverse so that the text will read correctly when transferred.

4. Use paper sparingly by ganging photos or text blocks together onto a single page using your computer's software.

5. Feed the paper into the printer with the paper side facing down or according to the manufacturer's instructions (*photo 3*). After the image has been printed onto the paper, remove the paper immediately and lay it faceup to allow it to dry.

6. Cut the images apart, leaving white space around the borders. With the image facing down, place the transfer-paper image on the fabric.

7. Transfer the images by laying them facedown on the desired fabrics and press using a hot iron. Using an iron at the hottest setting and without steam, press the iron firmly on the paper side of the image (*photo 2*). Press and hold the iron following the paper manufacturer's instructions; then lift and press another area of the paper. Continue pressing until you've covered all areas of the paper. Follow the manufacturer's instructions to peel the paper off when the paper is still hot or when it's cool.

Personalize a wall hanging with photo transfers pieced inside star blocks. When printing the transfers, print them in black-and-white for a timeless look.

my sister, my friend

DESIGNED BY KRIS KERRIGAN
PHOTOGRAPHED BY
HOPKINS ASSOCIATES

MATERIALS

⅓ yard of solid light yellow for blocks

¼ yard total of assorted bright yellow prints for blocks and flower appliqués

½ yard total of assorted dark purple prints for blocks and flower appliqués

½ yard of assorted bright pink prints for flower appliqués

¼ yard of green plaid for leaf appliqués

⅜ yard of green print for inner border and leaf appliqués

1 yard of purple-and-yellow print for outer border

¾ yard of purple plaid for cording

4½ yards of cording

1¼ yards of backing fabric

43" square of quilt batting

FINISHED QUILT TOP: 37" square
FINISHED STAR BLOCK: 12" square

Quantities specified for 44/45"-wide, 100% cotton fabrics.
All measurements include ¼" seam allowance unless otherwise stated.

CUT FABRICS

To make the best use of your fabrics, cut the pieces in the order that follows. To make templates of the appliqué patterns, found on *page 37*, follow the instructions in Quilting Basics on *page 44* for hand appliqué.

from solid light yellow, cut:
• 4—6½" squares
from assorted bright yellow prints, cut:
• 32—3½" squares
• 16 of Pattern A
from assorted dark purple prints, cut:
• 16—3½×6½" rectangles
• 16—3½" squares
• 16 of Pattern B
from assorted bright pink prints, cut:
• 16 of Pattern C
from green plaid, cut:
• 12 *each* of patterns E and E reversed
from green print, cut:
• 2—1×24½" inner border strips
• 2—1×25½" inner border strips
• 12 *each* of patterns D and D reversed
from purple-and-yellow print, cut:
• 4—6½×42" outer border strips
from purple plaid, cut:
• 1—25" square, cutting it into enough 2½"-wide bias strips to total 160" in length for cording.

ASSEMBLE STAR BLOCKS

1. For one star block you'll need one solid light yellow 6½" square with a photo transferred onto it, eight bright yellow print 3½" squares, four dark purple print 3½" squares, and four dark purple print 3½×6½" rectangles.

2. For accurate sewing lines, use a quilting pencil to mark each bright yellow print 3½" square with a diagonal line on the wrong side of the fabric. (To prevent your fabric from stretching as you draw the lines, place 220-grit sandpaper under the squares.)

3. With right sides together, align one marked bright yellow print square with one end of a dark purple print 3½×6½" rectangle (see Diagram 1; note the placement of the sewing line). Stitch on the sewing line; trim the seam allowance to ¼". Press open the attached yellow print triangle. Sew a second marked bright yellow print square to the opposite end of the rectangle; trim and press to make a Flying Geese unit (see Diagram 2). The Flying Geese unit should measure 3½×6½", including the seam allowances.

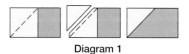

Diagram 1

Diagram 2
Make 4 Flying Geese units

my sister, my friend

4. Repeat Step 3 to make a total of four Flying Geese units.

5. Sew one Flying Geese unit to the top edge and one to the bottom edge of the solid light yellow 6½" square (see Diagram 3). Press the seam allowances toward the light yellow square. To each end of the remaining Flying Geese units, sew a dark purple print 3½" square. Press

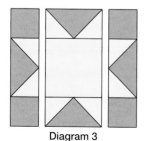
Diagram 3

the seam allowances toward the dark purple squares. Then join one pieced Flying Geese unit to each side edge of the light yellow square to complete the star block. Press the seam allowances toward the light yellow square. The pieced star block should measure 12½" square, including the seam allowances.

6. Repeat steps 1 through 5 for a total of four star blocks.

ASSEMBLE QUILT TOP

1. Referring to the photograph *above* for placement, lay out the pieced star blocks in two horizontal rows of two blocks each. Sew together the blocks in each row. Then join the rows. The pieced quilt top

should measure 24½" square, including the seam allowances.

2. Sew one green print 1×24½" inner border strip to the top edge and one to the bottom edge of the pieced quilt top. Then add one green print 1×25½" inner border strip to each side edge of the pieced quilt top. Press the seam allowances toward the green border.

3. Referring to the instructions for mitering corners in Quilting Basics on *page 44*, add the purple-and-yellow print 6½×42" outer border strips to the pieced quilt top, mitering corners.

APPLIQUÉ QUILT TOP

1. Prepare the pieces for appliqué by finger-pressing the 3/16" seam allowance under; you don't need to turn under edges that will be overlapped by other pieces.

2. Referring to the photograph *opposite* for placement, pin or hand-baste appliqué pieces to the purple-and-yellow print outer border. Begin with the pieces on the bottom and work up.

3. Using small slip stitches and threads in colors that match the fabrics, turn under the seam allowances as you appliqué the flowers and leaves to the background.

FINISH QUILT

1. Sew the purple plaid bias strips end to end to make one long bias strip.

2. With wrong sides together, fold under 1½" at one end of the bias strip. With wrong sides together, fold the bias strip in half lengthwise; press. Insert the cording between the bias strip layers next to the folded edge. Using a machine cording foot, sew through both bias strip layers right next to the cording.

3. Starting in the lower right-hand corner of the quilt top, align raw edges and stitch the covered cording to the right side of the top. Begin stitching 1½" from the cording's folded end. Your corners will be slightly rounded. As you stitch each corner, gently push the covered cording into place.

4. After going around the edge of the quilt top, cut the end of the cording so that it will fit snugly into the folded opening at the beginning. The ends of the cording should abut inside the purple plaid cover. Stitch the ends down and trim raw edges as needed.

5. Layer the quilt top, batting, and backing according to the instructions in Quilting Basics, which begins on *page 44*.

6. Quilt as desired. To finish the quilt, trim the batting even with the cording seam line. Trim the backing even with the outer raw edge of the quilt top, ¼" larger than the batting on all sides. Fold the backing over the batting. Fold under the cording cover's seam allowance; whipstitch edges together.

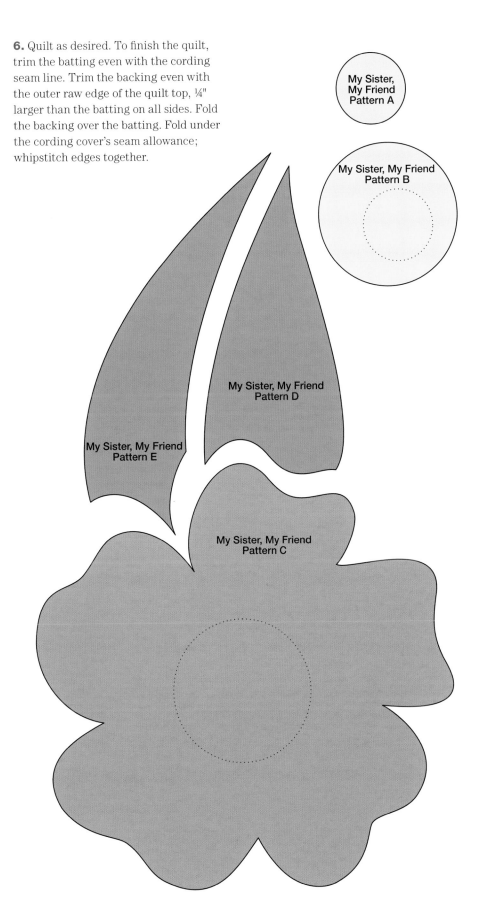

memories
in the making

Remember a special event or milestone with a unique photo-transfer quilt.

DESIGNED BY ELIZABETH TISINGER
PHOTOGRAPHED BY BLAINE MOATS

CAROL SUE
AND
ADAM DAVID

SEPTEMBER 4, 2005

DESIGNER NOTES

Before cutting your fabrics, transfer all photos and desired text onto the fabrics. Be sure to enlarge your photos so that there is enough room around the edges of the photo for cropping and seam allowances.

This quilt requires four photos with a horizontal orientation and four photos with a vertical orientation. The center block includes the names of the bride and groom along with their wedding date, and it was also printed onto printer fabric sheets.

CUT FABRICS

To make the best use of your fabrics, cut the pieces in the order that follows.

from muslin printed with photos or text, cut:
• 9—5½×8½" rectangles (four vertical, five horizontal)
from *each* assorted blue print, cut:
• 2—2½×8½" rectangles
from blue print, cut:
• 4—4×36" border strips
from light blue print, cut:
• 3—2½×42" binding strips

ASSEMBLE BLOCKS

1. Aligning long edges, sew two matching blue print 2½×8½" rectangles to a printed photo 5½×8½" rectangle to make block A (see Diagram 1). Press the seam allowances toward the blue print rectangles. Pieced block A should measure 9½" square, including the seam allowances. Repeat to make a total of 5 of block A.

Diagram 1

2. Aligning long edges, sew two matching blue print 2½×8½" rectangles to a printed photo 5½×8½" rectangle to make block B (see Diagram 2). Press the seam allowance toward the blue print rectangles. Pieced block B should measure 9½" square, including the seam allowances. Repeat to make a total of 4 of block B.

Diagram 2

ASSEMBLE QUILT CENTER

1. Referring to the photograph *opposite* for placement, lay out the nine blocks in three horizontal rows, alternating blocks A and B.

2. Sew together the blocks in each row. Press the seam allowances toward the A blocks.

3. Join the rows to make the quilt center. Press the seam allowances in one direction. The pieced quilt center should measure 27½" square, including the seam allowances.

ADD BORDERS

1. Fold each blue print border strip in half crosswise and press lightly to mark the center; unfold. Fold the assembled quilt center in half horizontally and vertically; press lightly to mark the center of each edge and unfold.

2. With right sides together and center marks and edges aligned, place a 4×36" border strip on each side edge of the quilt center. Sew together, beginning and ending ¼" from the end of the pieced center. *Note:* The remainder of the border strip is left free for mitering.

Repeat, joining the remaining blue print 4×43" border strips to opposite sides.

3. Miter the border corners to complete the quilt top. To miter corners, see Quilting Basics, which begins on *page 44*.

FINISH QUILT

1. Layer the quilt top, batting, and backing according to the instructions in Quilting Basics on *page 44*. Quilt as desired.

2. Use the blue print 2½×42" strips to bind the quilt according to the instructions in Quilting Basics.

stick to it

DESIGNED BY JEAN BAILEY
OF WILDCAT STUDIOS
PHOTOGRAPHED BY CAMERON
SADEGHPOUR AND SCOTT LITTLE

Have special photos but don't want to turn them into photo transfers? Frame your favorites with magnetic quilts.

DIAMOND BLOCK

STRIP-INSERTION BLOCK

DOUBLE-BORDER BLOCK

COURTHOUSE STEPS BLOCK

MATERIALS for one frame
(Refer to Select Materials and specific block instructions for more information.)

1¾x2½" to 2x3" photograph
Fabric scraps in assorted colors for block
8x12" rectangle of muslin for backing
8" square of lightweight cotton batting
8" square of stiff interfacing
2x5" flat magnet
Fine-tip permanent marking pen

FINISHED FRAMES:
6x6¼" (Courthouse Steps); 5x7" (Double-Border and Strip-Insertion); 6½" square (Diamond)

All measurements include a ¼" seam allowance. Sew with right sides together unless otherwise stated.

SELECT MATERIALS

Jean offers these tips for finding and choosing the necessary supplies to make your own fabric photo frames:

• The photos are actually stitched onto the frames. If you're concerned about using your only copy of a snapshot, scan the original photo and print it on photo paper at home, or have it duplicated by a professional.

• Purchase flat magnets at a crafts store or recycle your collection of advertising magnets. If you can't find the right-size magnet, tape two smaller magnets together and trim as necessary.

• Look for fabric color inspiration from the photo you're going to feature, then select colors to complement the photo. Or choose the favorite colors of the frame's recipient.

CUT AND ASSEMBLE COURTHOUSE STEPS BLOCK

from print No. 1, cut:
• 1—2½x3¾" rectangle for block center

from print No. 2, cut:
• 2—1½x3¾" rectangles for positions 1 and 2

from print No. 3, cut:
• 2—1¾x4½" rectangles for positions 3 and 4

from print No. 4, cut:
• 2—1¼x6¼" rectangles for positions 5 and 6

from photograph, cut:
• 1—1¾x2½" rectangle

Sew positions 1 and 2 rectangles to long edges of the 2½x3¾" block center. Press seams toward positions 1 and 2 rectangles. Referring to Diagram 1, continue adding rectangles in numerical order to make a Courthouse Steps block. Always press seams away from the center. The block should be 6x6¼", including seam allowances.

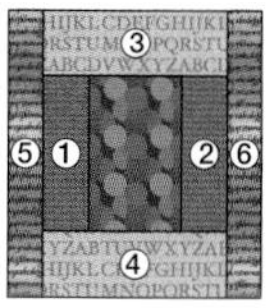

Diagram 1

CUT AND ASSEMBLE DOUBLE-BORDER BLOCK

from print No. 1, cut:
• 1—2½x3½" rectangle for block center

from print No. 2, cut:
• 2—1¼x5" inner border strips
• 2—1¼x2½" inner border strips

from print No. 3, cut:
• 2—1x7" outer border strips
• 2—1½x4" outer border strips

from photograph, cut:
• 1—1¾x2½" rectangle

Sew short inner border strips to short edges of the block center. Sew long inner border strips to remaining edges of block center. Press all seams toward inner border. Repeat to add outer border strips to block center to make the double-border block. The block should be 5x7", including seam allowances.

stick to it

CUT AND ASSEMBLE STRIP-INSERTION BLOCK

from print No. 1, cut:
• 1—6×8" rectangle

from print No. 2, cut:
• 2—1×8" strips

from photograph, cut:
• 1—1¾×2½" rectangle

1. Place an acrylic ruler at a slight angle on one corner of the print No. 1—6×8" rectangle (see Diagram 2). Cut across corner; save the resulting corner triangle.

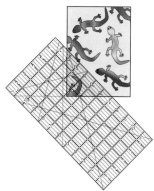

Diagram 2

2. Join a print No. 2—1×8" strip to the cut edge of the rectangle (see Diagram 3). Sew the corner triangle to the other edge of the print No. 2 strip (see Diagram 4). Press all seams toward the print No. 2 strip.

Diagram 3

Diagram 4

3. Repeat steps 1 and 2 to insert remaining print No. 2 strip on the opposite corner.

4. Trim the pieced rectangle to 5×7", including seam allowances, to complete the strip-insertion block.

CUT AND ASSEMBLE DIAMOND BLOCK

The Diamond Pattern is *opposite*. To make a template of the pattern, see Quilting Basics, which begins on *page 44*.

from print No. 1, cut:
• 1 of Diamond Pattern

from print No. 2, cut:
• 4—2½×7" strips
• 2—1¼×6½" strips

from print No. 3, cut:
• 2—1×6½" strips

from photograph, cut:
• 1—1¾×2½" rectangle

1. Join print No. 2—2½×7" strips to opposite sides of print No. 1 diamond. Trim strip edges even with diamond edges (see Diagram 5). Add 2½×7" strips to remaining edges to make a bordered diamond.

Diagram 5

2. Trim the bordered diamond to measure 4×6½" including the seam allowances (see Diagram 6).

Diagram 6

3. Join print No. 3—1×6½" strips to the side edges of the bordered diamond. Join print No. 2—1¼×6½" strips to side edges to make the diamond block (see Diagram 7). Press all seams toward outer edges. The block should be 6½" square, including seam allowances.

Diagram 7

FINISH FRAME

1. Layer a batting 8" square on a stiff interfacing 8" square, then center the pieced block on top.

2. Quilt as desired. Jean machine-quilted in the ditch of all seams. On some of her featured frames, she also stipple-quilted the block background, used decorative machine stitches to add more texture, or quilted around motifs in the fabric prints.

3. Place photograph in block center; use a small piece of double-stick tape to hold photo in place. Using a wide (4 mm) and long (2 mm) zigzag, machine-stitch around photograph. Allow the zigzag to fall about half on and half off the edge. Trim batting and interfacing even with block edges.

4. Fold under 2½" on one short end of the muslin 8×12" backing rectangle; topstitch in place close to the raw edge to make magnet pocket (see Diagram 8). With raw edge of pocket facing up, place quilted block right side up atop muslin backing rectangle; magnet pocket should align with top of the block. Pin muslin backing to block and trim even with block edges.

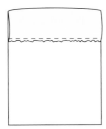

Diagram 8

5. Set up your sewing machine for a 4-mm-wide, 1-mm-long zigzag stitch. Starting at the upper left corner of the layered block, stitch clockwise around all edges; when you reach the left-hand side of the magnet pocket, slip magnet into pocket (see Diagram 9). Finish stitching to the upper edge to make the frame.

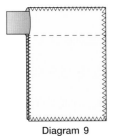

Diagram 9

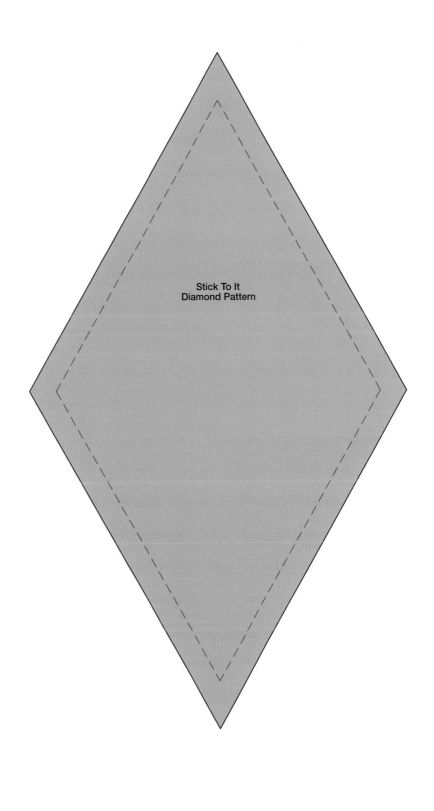

Stick To It
Diamond Pattern

quilting basics

Read through these general quilting instructions to ensure you'll properly cut and assemble your quilt. Accuracy in each step guarantees a successful quiltmaking experience.

TOOLS
cutting

Acrylic ruler: To aid in making perfectly straight cuts with a rotary cutter, choose a ruler of thick, clear plastic. Many sizes are available. A 6×24" ruler marked in ¼" increments with 30°, 45°, and 60° angles is a good first purchase.

Rotary-cutting mat: A rotary cutter should always be used with a mat designed specifically for it. In addition to protecting the table, the mat helps keep the fabric from shifting while you cut. Often these mats are described as self-healing, meaning the blade does not leave slash marks or grooves in the surface, even after repeated usage. While many shapes and styles are available, a 16×23" mat marked with a 1" grid, with hash marks at ⅛" increments, and 45° and 60° angles is a good choice.

Rotary cutter: The round blade of a rotary cutter will cut up to six layers of fabric at once. Because the blade is so sharp, be sure to purchase one with a safety guard and keep the guard over the blade when you're not cutting. The blade can be removed from the handle and replaced when it gets dull. Commonly available in three sizes, a good first blade is a 45 mm.

Scissors: You'll need one pair for cutting fabric and another for cutting paper and plastic.

Pencils and other marking tools: Marks made with special quilt markers are easy to remove after sewing.

Template plastic: This slightly frosted plastic comes in sheets about ¹⁄₁₆" thick.

PIECING

Iron and ironing board

Sewing thread: Use 100% cotton thread.

Sewing machine: Any machine in good working order with well-adjusted tension will produce pucker-free patchwork seams.

APPLIQUÉ

Fusible web: Instead of using the traditional method, secure cutout shapes to background of an appliqué block with this iron-on adhesive.

Hand-sewing needles: For hand appliqué, most quilters like fine quilting needles.

HAND QUILTING

Frame or hoop: You will get smaller, more even stitches if you stretch your quilt as you stitch. A frame supports the quilt's weight, ensures even tension, and frees your hands for stitching. However, once set up, it can't be disassembled until the quilting is complete. Quilting hoops are more portable and less expensive.

Quilting needles: A "between" or quilting needle is short with a small eye. Common sizes are 8, 9, and 10; size 8 is best for beginners.

Quilting thread: Quilting thread is stronger than sewing thread.

Thimble: This finger cover relieves the pressure required to push needle through several layers of fabric and batting.

MACHINE QUILTING

Darning foot: You may find this tool, also called a hopper foot, in your sewing machine's accessory kit. If not, have the model and brand of your machine available when you got to purchase one. It is used for free-motion stitching.

Safety pins: They hold the layers together during quilting.

Table: Use a large work surface that is level with your machine bed.

Thread: Use 100% cotton quilting thread, cotton-wrapped polyester quilting thread, or very fine nylon monofilament thread.

Walking foot: This sewing-machine accessory helps you keep long, straight quilting lines smooth and pucker-free.

CHOOSE YOUR FABRICS

Most patterns, including those in this book, specify quantities for 44/45"-wide fabrics unless otherwise noted. Our projects call for a little extra yardage in length to allow for minor errors and slight shrinkage.

PREPARE YOUR FABRICS

We recommend you prewash a scrap of each fabric to test it for shrinkage and bleeding. If you choose to prewash an entire fabric piece, unfold it to a single layer. Wash it in warm water, which will allow the fabric to shrink and/or bleed. If the fabric bleeds, rinse it until the water runs clear. Do not use it in a quilt if it hasn't stopped bleeding. Hang the fabric to dry, or tumble it in the dryer until slightly damp; press well.

SELECT THE BATTING

For a small beginner project, a thin cotton batting is a good choice. It has a tendency to "stick" to fabric so it requires less basting. Also, it's easy to stitch. It's wise to follow the stitch density (distance between rows of stitching required to keep the batting from shifting and wadding up inside the quilt) recommendation printed on the packaging.

Polyester batting is lightweight and readily available. In general, it springs back to its original height when compressed, adding a puffiness to quilts. It tends to "beard" (work out between the weave of the fabric) more than natural fibers. Polyester fleece is denser and works well for pillow tops and place mats.

Wool batting has good loft retention and absorbs moisture, making it ideal for cool, damp climates. Read the label carefully before purchasing a wool batting because it may require special handling.

CUTTING BIAS STRIPS

Strips for curved appliqué pattern pieces and for binding curved edges should be cut on the bias (diagonally across the grain of a woven fabric), which runs at a 45° angle to the selvage and has the most stretch.

To cut bias strips, begin with a fabric square or rectangle; use an acrylic ruler to square up the left edge. Make a cut at a 45° angle to the left edge (see Bias Strip Diagram *below*). Handle the diagonal edges carefully to avoid distorting the bias. To cut a strip, measure the desired width from the 45° cut edge; cut parallel to the edge. Cut enough strips to total the length needed.

Bias Strip Diagram

MAKE TEMPLATES

A template is a pattern made from sturdy material so you can trace around it many times without wearing away the edges. Acrylic templates for many common shapes are available at quilt shops. Or, you can make your own by duplicating printed patterns on plastic.

To make permanent templates, try using easy-to-cut template plastic, available at crafts supply stores. This material lasts indefinitely, and its transparency allows you to trace the pattern directly onto its surface.

To make a template, lay the plastic over a printed pattern. Trace the pattern onto the plastic using a ruler and a permanent marker. This will ensure straight lines, accurate corners, and permanency.

For hand piecing and appliqué, make templates the exact size the finished pieces will be, without seam allowances, by tracing the patterns' dashed lines.

For machine piecing, make templates that include the seam allowances.

For easy reference, mark each template with its letter designation, grain line if noted, and block name. Verify the template's size by placing it over the printed pattern. Templates must be accurate or the error, however small, will compound many times as you assemble a quilt. To check the accuracy of your templates, make a test block before cutting the fabric pieces for an entire quilt.

TRACE TEMPLATES

To mark on fabric, use a pencil, white dressmaker's pencil, chalk, or a special fabric marker that makes a thin, accurate line. Do not use a ballpoint or ink pen; it may bleed if washed. Test all marking tools on a fabric scrap before using them.

To trace pieces that will be used for hand piecing or appliqué, place templates facedown on the wrong side of the fabric; position the templates at least ½" apart (see Diagram 1). The traced lines on the fabric are the sewing lines. Mark cutting lines ¼" away from the

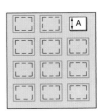

Diagram 1

sewing lines, or estimate the distance by eye when cutting out the pieces. For hand piecing, add a ¼" seam allowance; for hand appliqué, add a ³⁄₁₆" seam allowance.

Templates used to make pieces for machine piecing have seam allowances included so you can use common lines for efficient cutting. Place a template facedown on the wrong side of the fabric and trace; repeat, but do not leave spaces between the tracings (see Diagram 2). Using a rotary cutter and ruler, cut precisely on the drawn lines.

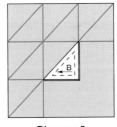

Diagram 2

PLAN FOR CUTTING

Our project instructions list pieces in the order they should be cut to make the best use of your fabrics. Always consider the fabric grain before cutting. The arrow on a pattern piece indicates which direction the fabric grain should run. One or more straight sides of the pattern piece should follow the fabric's lengthwise or crosswise grain.

The lengthwise grain, parallel to the selvage (the tightly finished edge), has the least amount of stretch. The crosswise grain, perpendicular to the selvage, has a little more give. The edge of any pattern piece that will be

quilting basics

on the outside of a block or quilt should always be cut on the lengthwise grain. Do not use the selvage of a woven fabric in a quilt. When washed, it may shrink more than the rest of the fabric.

In projects larger than 42" in length or width, we specify that the border strips be cut the width (crosswise grain) of the fabric and pieced to use the least amount of fabric. If you'd prefer to cut the border strips on the lengthwise grain and not piece them, you'll need to refigure the yardage.

COVERED CORDING
Covered cording is made by sewing a fabric strip around a length of cording. The width of the strip will vary depending on the diameter of your cording. Refer to the specific project instructions for those measurements. Regardless, the method used to cover the cording is the same.

With the wrong sides inside, fold the strip in half lengthwise to make the cording cover. Insert the cording next to the folded edge. Using a zipper or cording foot, sew through both layers right next to the cording (see Diagram 3).

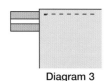

Diagram 3

MITERING BORDERS
To add a border with mitered corners, first pin a border strip to a quilt top edge, matching the center of the strip and the center of the quilt top edge. Sew together, beginning and ending the seam ¼" from the quilt top corners (see Diagram 3). Allow excess border fabric to extend beyond the edges. Repeat with remaining border strips. Press the seam allowances toward the border strips.

At one corner, lap one border strip over the other (see Diagram 4). Align the edge of a 90° right triangle with the raw edge of the top strip so the long edge of the triangle intersects the border seam in the corner. With a pencil, draw along the edge of the triangle from the seam out to the raw edge. Place the bottom border strip on top and repeat the marking process.

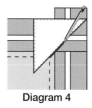

Diagram 4

With the right sides together, match the marked seam lines and pin (see Diagram 5).

Beginning with a backstitch at the inside corner, sew together the strips, stitching exactly on the marked lines. Check the right side to see that the corner lies flat. Trim the excess fabric, leaving a ¼" seam allowance. Press the seam open. Mark and sew the remaining corners in the same manner.

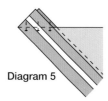

Diagram 5

COMPLETE THE QUILT
Cut and piece the backing fabric to measure at least 3" bigger on all sides than the quilt top. Press all seam allowances open. With wrong sides together, layer the quilt top and backing fabric with the batting in between; baste. Quilt as desired.

The binding for most quilts is cut on the straight grain of the fabric. If your quilt has curved edges, cut the strips on the bias (see *page 45*). The cutting instructions for projects

in this issue specify the number of binding strips or a total length needed to finish the quilt. The instructions also specify enough width for a French-fold, or double-layer, binding because it's easier to apply and adds durability.

Join the binding strips with diagonal seams (see Diagram 6) to make one continuous binding strip. Trim the excess fabric, leaving ¼" seam allowances. Press the seam allowances open. With the wrong side inside, fold under 1" at one end of the binding strip (see Diagram 7); press. Fold strip in half lengthwise (see Diagram 8).

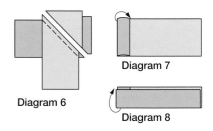

Diagram 7

Diagram 6

Diagram 8

Beginning in the center of one side, place the binding strip against the right side of the quilt top, aligning the binding strip's raw edges with the quilt top's raw edge (see Diagram 9 *opposite*). Sew through all layers, stopping ¼" from the corner (or a distance equal to the seam allowance you're using). Backstitch, then clip the threads. Remove the quilt from under the sewing-machine presser foot.

Fold the binding strip upward (see Diagram 10 *opposite*), creating a diagonal fold, and finger-press.

Holding the diagonal fold in place with your finger, bring the binding strip down in line with the next edge, making a horizontal fold that aligns with the quilt edge (see Diagram 11 *opposite*).

Start sewing again at the top of the horizontal fold, stitching through all layers. Sew around the quilt, turning each corner in the same manner.

When you return to the starting point, encase the binding strip's raw edge inside the folded end (see Diagram 12). Finish sewing to the starting point (see Diagram 13). Trim the batting and backing fabric even with the quilt top edges.

Turn the binding over the edge to the back. Hand-stitch the binding to the backing fabric, making sure to cover any machine stitching.

To make mitered corners on the back, hand-stitch up to a corner; fold a miter in the binding. Take a stitch or two in the fold to secure it. Then stitch the binding in place up to the next corner. Finish each corner in the same manner.

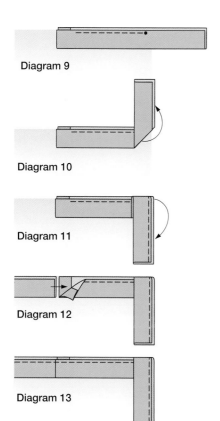

Diagram 9

Diagram 10

Diagram 11

Diagram 12

Diagram 13

HANGING SLEEVES

Quilts make wonderful pieces of wall art. When treated as museum pieces and hung properly, they won't deteriorate. Let size be your guide when determining how to hang your quilt.

Hang smaller quilts, a 25" square or less, with purchased clips, sewn-on tabs, or pins applied to the corners. Larger quilts require a hanging sleeve attached to the back. It may take a few mintues more to sew on a sleeve, but the effort preserves your hours of work with less distortion and damage.

Measure the quilt's top edge. Cut a 6"- to 10"-wide strip of prewashed fabric 2" longer than the quilt's top edge. For example, if the top edge is 40", cut a 6×42" strip. A 6"-wide strip is sufficient for a dowel or drapery rod. If you're using something bigger in diameter, cut a wider fabric strip. If you're sending your quilt to be displayed at a quilt show, adjust your measurements to accommodate the show's requirements. Fold under 1½" on both short ends of the fabric strip. Sew ¼" from the raw edges (see Diagram 14). Fold the fabric strip in half lengthwise with the wrong side inside; pin. Stitch together the long edges with a ¼" seam allowance (see Diagram 15) to make the sleeve. Press the seam allowance open and

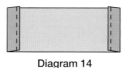

Diagram 14

Diagram 15

center the seam in the middle of the sleeve (see Diagram 16). Center the sleeve on the quilt backing (see Diagram 17). Stitching through the backing and batting, slip-stitch the sleeve to the quilt along both long edges and the portions of the short edges that touch the backing. Slide in a wooden dowel or slender piece of wood that is 1" longer than the finished sleeve; hang as desired.

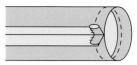

Diagram 16

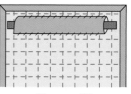

Diagram 17

Better Homes and Gardens®
Creative Collection™

Editorial Director John Riha

Editor in Chief Deborah Gore Ohrn

Executive Editor Karman Wittry Hotchkiss

Managing Editor Kathleen Armentrout

Contributing Editorial Manager Heidi Palkovic

Contributing Design Director Tracy DeVenney

Copy Chief Mary Heaton
Contributing Copy Editor Mary Helen Schiltz
Proofreader Joleen Ross
Administrative Assistant Lori Eggers

Publishing Group President
Jack Griffin

President and CEO Stephen M. Lacy

Chairman of the Board William T. Kerr

In Memoriam
E. T. Meredith III (1933–2003)